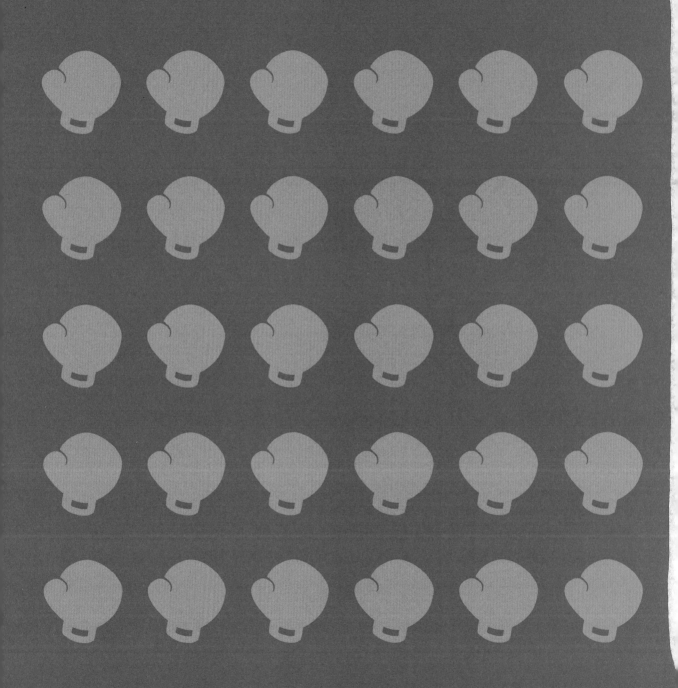

ORDINARY
PEOPLE
CHANGE
— THE —
WORLD

# I am Muhammad Ali

## BRAD MELTZER

### illustrated by Christopher Eliopoulos

DIAL BOOKS FOR YOUNG READERS

I am **MUHAMMAD ALI.**

From the day I was born, I've been loud and proud.
In the hospital, my cries would wake up all the other babies.

My parents named me Cassius Clay, Jr.
It was a name that came from the family who enslaved
my great-grandfather John Henry Clay.
You'll see why I changed it.

As a baby, I could never sit still.

In my stroller, I'd stand up to see everything, always looking for adventure.

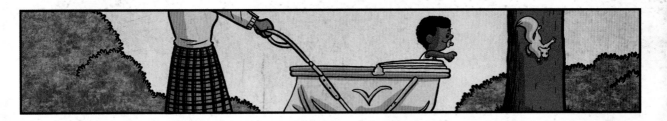

When I was a toddler, I accidentally knocked my mom's tooth loose.

Those first syllables I used to say—Gee-Gee—became my nickname, though my mom joked it meant Golden Gloves.

My mom was always proud, showing me so much love.

She really was the greatest.

Sadly, my hometown of Louisville, Kentucky, was segregated. That means Black people had different schools and different restaurants from white people, all of them worse than the ones in white neighborhoods.

One hot day when I was little, I was so thirsty, my mom asked if I could get a cup of water.

I cried the whole way home. I didn't understand why someone would hate us just because of our skin color.

It was the same at our local amusement park. Only white people could go on the rides. Since we were Black, we weren't allowed in.

My mother taught us that hating is wrong, no matter who does the hating.

At twelve years old, I got a new bike for Christmas and wanted to show it off.

When it started to rain and we got hungry, we headed for the local Black Home Show at a nearby gym.

When we got out, I discovered my bike was stolen!

Someone told me there was a police officer downstairs who could help.

I cried the entire way.

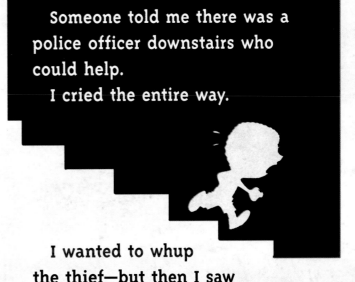

I wanted to whup the thief—but then I saw what was actually down there...

It was a moment
I'd never forget.

The sound of skipping ropes...

and gloves hitting bags.

FFF
FFF
FFF

THWAP
THWAP
THWAP

One boy was shadowboxing so fast, his hands were a blur.

And since both Black and white boxers were welcome,

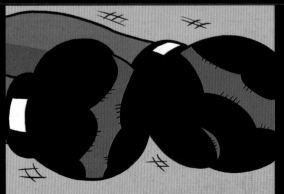

the outside world seemed to fade away.

Officer Martin was the one who asked me if I wanted to join the gym.
I was skinny and had never worn a pair of boxing gloves.
A few days later, I jumped into the ring with an older boy.
Within a minute, I had a bloody nose.

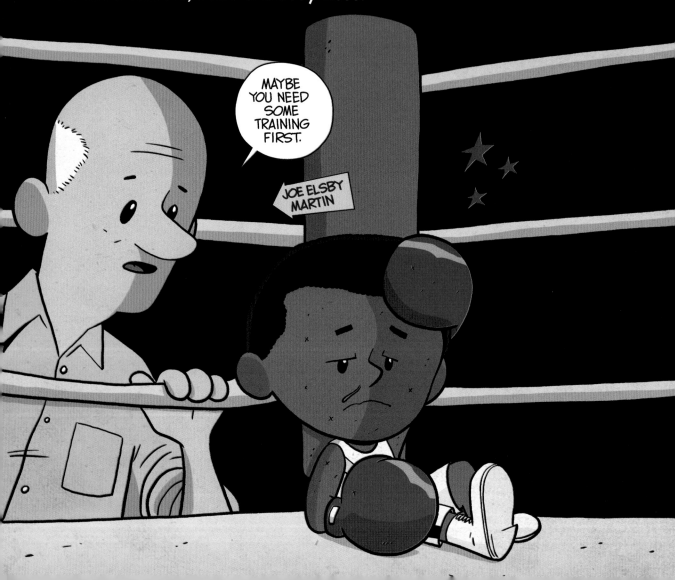

He was right.
To get faster, I'd race the school bus to school.

Officer Martin said I was an ordinary kid—that as a boxer, I had a lot to learn—but what made me stand out was my determination: It was impossible to discourage me.

One of my earliest fights was against a local bully named Corky Baker. We called him King of the Streets, since if you walked by him, you'd have to pay a "toll."

Corky was so tough, he once held a football player upside down to shake money from his pockets.

I knew I couldn't go far in boxing until I beat him.

He would've destroyed me if I fought him without rules.
So I convinced him to come to where I'd have the advantage...

Inside the ring.
I couldn't picture myself as a real champion until I stood up to Corky.

Was I scared?
Of course I was.
I hoped he wouldn't notice my knees shaking.

I let him throw a lot of punches to tire him out.
Before the second round was over, he ran out of the ring.

After that, Corky stopped bullying people.
He even shook my hand and told me I'd go a long way as a fighter.
But the most important thing I did that day was face my fears.

Today, people know me for my confidence.
But I was shy.
And I had something called dyslexia, which meant I had a hard time reading and interpreting words.

Before every big fight, I'd be so nervous, I'd throw up.

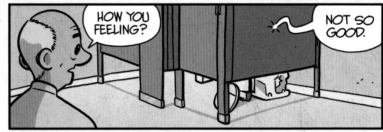

When I made it to the Olympics, I was even afraid to fly on a plane.
I bought a parachute and wore it the whole way.

But my father told me: Always confront the things you fear.
So when that boxing bell rang...

In 1960, at eighteen years old, I won the gold medal at the Olympics.

I thought winning the Olympic gold medal would change my life.
I wore it everywhere, figuring *now* they'd let me eat downtown.

America was supposed
to be the land of the free,
But *I* wasn't free.
Because of my skin
color, I didn't have the
same rights as others.

What I remember
most about that
year was taking *off*
my gold medal.

I went to Miami to become a professional fighter. During my morning runs, police would stop me because I was Black, calling my gym to verify I was really training there.

Soon after, I became a Muslim.
That means my religion is Islam.
We believe all humans are fighting for the
same things: love, unity, and understanding.

I kept my new religion to myself.
Back then, Black athletes weren't supposed to
talk about their beliefs.
We were supposed to be entertaining and thankful.
We were supposed to be quiet.

That wasn't my style.

When I'd introduce myself to people, I'd tell them:
"I'm going to be the heavyweight champion of the world."

My big personality helped me get attention, and soon,
I was set to fight the heavyweight champ.

He was one of the best fighters of all time, but he
hadn't fought *me*.

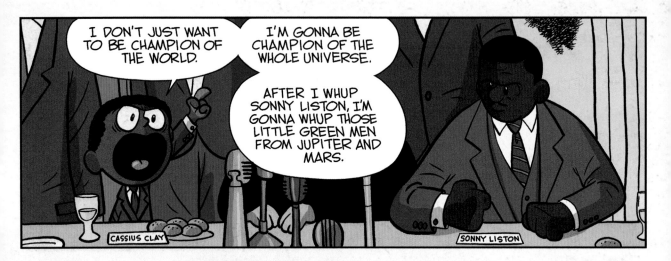

People think boxing is a brutal sport.
I turned it into a science.
I studied how Liston fought.

No one thought I would win.
But c'mon—*you* know what happened.

The next day, at the press conference, a reporter brought up my religion, asking if I was really Muslim.

I told him all I wanted was peace, but I knew he was questioning my beliefs.

Right there, I declared my independence.

Sometimes it's hard to stand up for what you believe—but that's always worth fighting for.

Soon after, I took on a new name.

Cassius Clay was the name of a white man—a slave owner—representing hundreds of years of injustice.

So I changed my name to *Muhammad Ali*, which meant *worthy of all praise.*

Sometimes, people didn't like when I spoke my mind.

But I was just telling the truth.

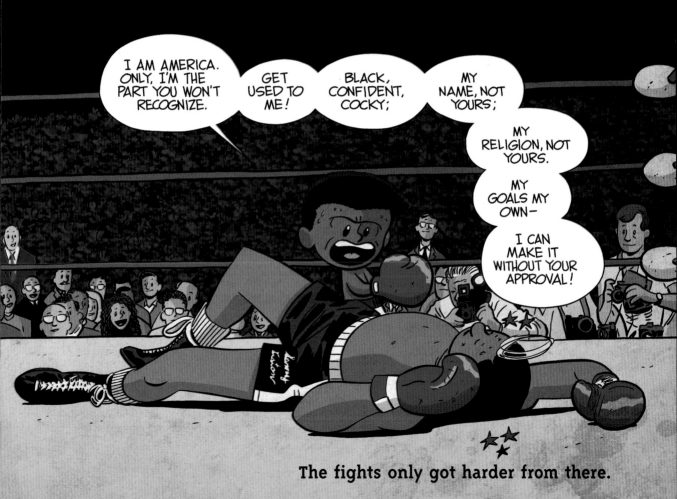

The fights only got harder from there.

The United States government used to be able to make you join the military.

They wanted me to fight a war in the country of Vietnam.

As a Muslim, though, I didn't believe in war.

Protesters called me "unpatriotic."

They said I should "Love America—or leave it."

It got even worse when I started speaking out about racism.

WHY ARE MORE BLACK SOLDIERS DYING THAN WHITE ONES?

HOW IS IT FAIR TO SEND ME THOUSANDS OF MILES AWAY TO ATTACK VIETNAMESE PEOPLE, WHEN BLACK PEOPLE HERE CAN'T EVEN EAT IN A RESTAURANT?

HE'S GOT A POINT.

For a while, I was the most hated man in America.

But in time, instead of protesting *against* me, people started protesting against the *war*—and *for* me.

ALI IS RIGHT!

THIS WAR IN VIETNAM IS WRONG!

SEND ME TO JAIL IF YOU WANT.

ALL I WANT IS JUSTICE.

The government eventually put me on trial for refusing to fight in the Vietnam War.

The jury said I was guilty.

I lost my championship title.

They wouldn't let me fight for three and a half years.

But when the Supreme Court—the biggest court in the country—finally heard the case, they agreed with *me*.

Over time, more and more people realized the war was wrong.

And I got the title no man or government could ever take away:

I was *The People's Champion.*

Eventually, I got in the ring again.
I didn't win every match.
But when I lost, I always got back up.

My greatest match took me to Zaire in Africa.
I was facing the new world champion, George Foreman.
But I was really facing my history—the continent where
my ancestors were enslaved, and a country where Black Africans
were still struggling to be free.
This time, though, I wasn't fighting alone.

The fight was seen by nearly a billion people, the most watched live TV event ever at the time.

Foreman was younger, stronger, and had never lost a fight.

C'MON, ALI!

YOU CAN DO IT, ALI!

GO, ALI!

ALI, BOMAYE!

ALI! ALI! ALI!

ONCE AGAIN, HEAVYWEIGHT CHAMPION OF THE WORLD!

I knew I wouldn't be able to outpunch him.

But as long as I stayed on my feet, I could certainly outlast him.

Who do you think won?

GO, ALI!

ALI!

LET'S GO, ALI!

C'MON, ALI!

YOU'VE GOT THIS, ALI!

I AM...

When I told you *I am America*, it's because my story
is an American story—and it's one that still continues.
The battle against racism isn't finished.
We all need to help.

They'll tell you to be quiet.
Don't be.
SPEAK UP! USE YOUR VOICE!
It's the only way we win the fight for justice.

In my life, people tried to knock me down.
They tried to count me out.
But my biggest fights weren't in a ring.
They were for principles—for things I believed in.
Was I scared?
I was *plenty* scared.
I just didn't let it stop me.

Anyone can pick a fight—but that doesn't make you strong.
Real strength comes from being true to your beliefs,
and being willing to lose everything for
what you think is right.
When you do that...

When the world knocks you down, get back up.
Keep fighting, even when you want to quit.
In those moments, you'll find your strength.

Want to be a champion?
Here's the secret.
It's not about who's stronger.

It's about who has the energy,
the determination,
the sheer will
to make their way to victory.

I am Muhammad Ali,
and I will always fight for what I believe in.

*"I hated every minute of training, but I said, 'Don't quit. Suffer now and live the rest of your life as a champion.'"*
—MUHAMMAD ALI

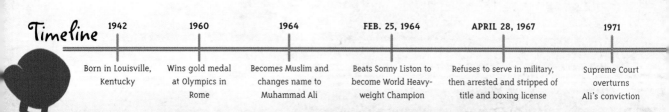

*Timeline*

| 1942 | 1960 | 1964 | FEB. 25, 1964 | APRIL 28, 1967 | 1971 |
|------|------|------|---------------|----------------|------|
| Born in Louisville, Kentucky | Wins gold medal at Olympics in Rome | Becomes Muslim and changes name to Muhammad Ali | Beats Sonny Liston to become World Heavyweight Champion | Refuses to serve in military, then arrested and stripped of title and boxing license | Supreme Court overturns Ali's conviction |

Muhammad at age twelve

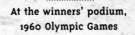

At the winners' podium,
1960 Olympic Games

Muhammad and his wife,
Lonnie, 1999

In Egypt, 1964

Dodging Joe Frazier's
punch, 1971

| OCTOBER 30, 1973 | 1984 | 1996 | 2005 | JUNE 3, 2016 | 2019 |
|---|---|---|---|---|---|
| Rumble in the Jungle against George Foreman | Diagnosed with Parkinson's disease | Lights Olympic torch at Atlanta Olympic Games | Awarded Presidential Medal of Freedom and opened the Muhammad Ali Center | Dies in Phoenix, Arizona | Louisville Airport named after him |

For Saif Ishoof,
beloved community leader
and treasured friend,
who has never been afraid to jump in the ring
–B.M.

For Michael J. Fox,
whose work I enjoy,
but whose life I admire.
"If you put your mind to it,
you can accomplish anything."
–C.E.

For historical accuracy, we used Muhammad Ali's actual words whenever possible. For more of his true voice, we recommend and acknowledge the below titles. Special thanks to Jeanie Kahnke and all our friends at the Muhammad Ali Center for their input on early drafts. Go visit them and see more at AliCenter.org.

· · · · · · · · · · · · · · · · · · · · · · · · · · · · · · · · · · · · · · · · · · · · · · · · · · · · · · · · · · · ·

## SOURCES

*The Greatest: My Own Story* by Muhammad Ali with Richard Durham (Random House, 1975)

*The Soul of a Butterfly: Reflections on Life's Journey* by Muhammad Ali with Hana Yasmeen Ali (Simon & Schuster, 2004)

*Ali: A Life* by Jonathan Eig (Simon & Schuster, 2017)

*Muhammad Ali: His Life and Times* by Thomas Hauser (Simon & Schuster, 1991)

*My Brother, Muhammad Ali: The Definitive Biography* by Rahaman Ali with Fiaz Rafiq (Rowman & Littlefield, 2020)

## FURTHER READING FOR KIDS

*Who Was Muhammad Ali?* by James Buckley Jr. (Penguin Workshop, 2014)

*What Was the Vietnam War?* by Jim O'Connor (Penguin Workshop, 2019)

*Muhammad Ali Visual Encyclopedia* (DK, 2018)

· · · · · · · · · · · · · · · · · · · · · · · · · · · · · · · · · · · · · · · · · · · · · · · · · · · · · · · · · · · ·

DIAL BOOKS FOR YOUNG READERS
An imprint of Penguin Random House LLC, New York

First published in the United States of America by Dial Books for Young Readers, an imprint of Penguin Random House LLC, 2022

Text copyright © 2022 by Forty-four Steps, Inc. • Illustrations copyright © 2022 by Christopher Eliopoulos

Dial and colophon are registered trademarks of Penguin Random House LLC.

Visit us online at penguinrandomhouse.com.

Library of Congress Cataloging-in-Publication Data is available.

Photo on page 38 courtesy of Francesco Da Vinci/Archive Photos/Getty Images. Photos on page 39: Muhammad Ali at age twelve courtesy of Bettmann Archive/Getty Images; winners' podium courtesy of Central Press/Stringer/Getty Images; in Egypt courtesy of RDB/ullstein bild/Getty Images; Ali vs Frazier courtesy of Bettmann Archive/Getty Images; and Muhammad and Lonnie Ali courtesy of Steve Liss/The LIFE Images Collection/Getty Images.

ISBN 9780593405857 • Printed in the United States of America • 10 9 8 7 6 5 4 3 2 1

PC

Designed by Jason Henry • Text set in Triplex • The artwork for this book was created digitally.